Tennessee's Crisis of Individual Over-Incarceration.

Tut Mayal Tut

TABLE OF CONTENTS

DEDICATION PAGE

In loving memory of Duol T. Wal

Flesh of my flesh

My battle-tested soldier

The man I came into this struggle with

PREFACE

At year-end 2016, about 18% of Tennessee's prisoners were serving sentences that effectively guarantee death while incarcerated. I'm referring to life with parole sentences, life without parole sentences, and virtual life sentences-sentences that require service of at least 50 years of confinement according to the D.C. Sentencing Project. Fast forward 7 years and that number has without a doubt increased, especially since the state has shifted towards the harsher end of the sentencing pendulum through its most recent criminal justice legislation. Nevertheless, the incarcerated population in need of attention is broader than this particular demographic. In my opinion, anyone serving a sentence that requires service of at least 20 years of confinement runs the risk of becoming a victim of what I call individual over-incarceration, which is the warehousing of prisoners above and beyond a reasonable degree of punishment and rehabilitation. Upon my arrival in the Department of Correction, I quickly realized that long-term prisoners possessed a wealth of knowledge relative to the system that needed to be synthesized. From the lives and intellects of hundreds of prisoners, I've learned why contemporary confinement and release practices within Tennessee's legal system continuously backfire. Being incarcerated myself, I'm also acquainted with the adverse effects that these practices imprint upon the attitudes that incarcerated people have towards self improvement. All of this prompted me to come up with ideas that have the potential to improve upon our criminal justice failings. Equipped with this empirical information I decided to voice these ideas that emanate from the people that are primarily affected by individual over-incarceration; long-term prisoners serving lengthy sentences who sincerely strive to get their lives in order. Perhaps those within the state power structure will consider this perspective and come up with a way to re-distribute release opportunities to the '*right*' prisoners. Even if they happen to be serving major sentences for major crimes.

INTRODUCTION

I think it's safe to say that most prisoners couldn't care less about the pontification of self-proclaimed social justice advocates who write books, give lectures, and make television appearances for the sake of presenting their elaborate words on mass incarceration, bail reform, and prison overcrowding. We're also driven crazy by the public obsession with police and police tactics as if they're the end-all and be-all of the criminal justice system. The truth is that America will never get rid of the police! Who're the well-to-do going to call when they feel that their communities are being infiltrated? Who're the elderly going to rely on when they're carjacked in broad daylight in the midst of our all too common indifference? Who's going to respond when a gunman with military artillery initiates the next mass shooting, giving more numbers to this country's *'preventable'* body count? Excuse my sarcasm, but I'm willing to bet that it's going to be the "God-damned!" police. From the viewpoint of prisoners serving extensive sentences, I'm here to let it be known that public attention needs to be re-directed in order to diffuse the indifference towards re-assessing the condition of prisoners who've served decades worth of time on their sentences. This is a necessary order of business if we ever happen to generate the inclination to tackle the obstacles that prevent the release of men and women who've been rotting within the system for 20, 30, and 40 years or more... people who've paid the price for crime and have become paragons of development, although their light is stifled by a system that seems to let out all the *'wrong'* people. The long overdue objective here then is to address 2 tactics that are used in Tennessee's penal system to over-incarcerate those who've been found guilty of crimes. It's my belief that even when incarceration is just, there comes a time when the abatement of punishment should become an option.

I've been in prison since I was a child, so I see things from a unique perspective. When most people I meet think of recidivism, there is a tendency to fixate on 2 questions: "What services can be provided to offenders that are on the brink of release?" and "Why do repeat offenders re-offend?" To hell with those questions. On behalf of prisoners who've done a lot of time I say that resources and research needs to be geared towards uncovering the characteristics of the 20% or so that get out never to return to prison. When this is done, opportunities at release can be re-distributed to the *'right'* people; those who've managed to become accomplished albeit in shackles. In other words, incarcerated people who do the same things that were done by ex-prisoners who successfully transition back into society ought to be identified and rewarded. You might think to yourself at this point, *'People who end up with lengthy sentences are the most dangerous criminals who pose a threat to society.'* There's some truth to that idea. Prior to arrest and in their early years of confinement, many people who fall into lives of crime conduct themselves in a manner that warrants apprehension. The fallacy to the thought comes in when we accord incorrigibility to people under the simplistic notion that *'people are who they are'* as if growth is an impossibility for criminals. In my years in prison, I've observed that the on-the-ground reality is that convicts who face the most serious consequences tend to respond with the most seriousness towards doing what needs to be done to cherish their freedom and be successful post-release. With this fact in mind, it's important to ask ourselves if it makes sense to deny 2nd chances to people who can perceive the value of freedom and the rights of other citizens even though they may have a boatload of time.

In the subsequent pages, the primary obstacles that have led to Tennessee's over-incarceration crisis will be assessed. Furthermore, readers will get a snapshot of the people who're affected by these issues. I don't have the capacity to analyze every real life over-incarceration story, so I've simply given readers enough stories here to get the message. The 2 factors in question are as follows: (1) **'Offense Seriousness'** as enumerated under T.C.A 40-35-503 and (2) **'Extensive Sentences'** that lack meaningful mechanisms for rewarding rehabilitation. If criminal justice reform advocates and lawmakers absorb the contents of this booklet with clear minds, over-incarceration and recidivism can be diminished significantly. The importance of finding a solution that gives life to the *'right'* prisoners without sacrificing accountability can't be overstated. As a prisoner serving a 30-year sentence while committed to abandoning a life of crime I live the life of a fish out of water on a daily basis. I'm sure thousands of other prisoners feel the same way as we attempt to pick up the pieces in an environment full of fear, chaos, and desperation.... an environment where we can only hope for help as we act on our commitment for change.

SECTION 1

The People Who're Over-Incarcerated

On the pretext of '*Offense Seriousness*'

A COMMON OBSTACLE FOR PRISONERS

In the state of Tennessee, one of the many considerations that's traditionally applied by members of the parole board when making determinations as to who's granted parole or given a recommendation for sentence commutation, executive clemency, etc. is the seriousness of an offense. This concept is explained under the following 2 state legal statutes. I give them hereunder as they are written:

TN Administrative Code 1100-01-01-.07. *Board Criteria for Granting or Denying Parole*. Section (4)(b):

(4) After applying the various factors for consideration to the individual inmate, the Board shall deny the inmate's release on parole if it determines that:

(b) Release from custody at this time would depreciate the **seriousness of the crime** of which the person stands convicted or promote disrespect for the law; ...

As well as per T.C.A 40-35-503. *Release Status; Determinations*. Section (b)-(2)(A) & (B):

(b) Release on parole is a privilege and not a right, and no inmate convicted shall be granted parole if the board finds that:

(2)(A) The release from custody at the time would depreciate the **seriousness of the crime** of which the incarcerated individual stands convicted or promote disrespect for the law, except that the board's finding shall not be the sole basis for denying parole unless the individual is serving a sentence for any of the following offenses, in which case the board may deny parole for **seriousness of the offense**:

I. First Degree murder or an attempt to commit, solicitation of, or facilitation of first-degree murder;

II. Second Degree murder or an attempt to commit, solicitation of, or facilitation of second-degree murder;

III. Voluntary manslaughter

IV. Aggravated vehicular homicide;

V. Vehicular homicide

VI. Especially aggravated kidnapping or an attempt to commit or facilitation of especially aggravated kidnapping;

VII. Trafficking for a commercial sex act;

VIII. A human trafficking offense;

IX. Advertising commercial sexual abuse of a minor;

X. Especially aggravated robbery or an attempt to commit or facilitation of especially aggravated robbery;

XI. Aggravated rape of a child or an attempt to commit or facilitation of aggravated rape of a child;

XII. Aggravated rape or an attempt to commit or facilitation of aggravated rape;

XIII. Rape of a child or an attempt to commit or facilitation of rape of a child;

XIV. Rape;

XV. Aggravated sexual battery;

XVI. Especially aggravated burglary;

XVII. Aggravated child abuse;

XVIII. Aggravated sexual exploitation of a minor;

XIX. Especially aggravated sexual exploitation of a minor;

XX. Aggravated vehicular assault;

XXI. Aggravated abuse of an elderly or vulnerable adult; or

XXII. Vehicular assault

(B) If the board denies parole for the **seriousness of the offense**, then the board shall state in writing how the inmate can improve the inmate's chances of being released on parole at the inmate's next hearing; …

(***Note**: These statutes can be misleading due to the reality that many of the sex offenses listed above are parole ineligible. The 2 above-mentioned statutes convey the sense that they prevent child abusers and some of the most dangerous sex offenders from re-entry into society whereas under T.C.A statute those convicted of sex offenses must serve 100% of their sentences without parole consideration or the opportunity of earning sentence reduction credits, what people familiar with corrections usually call "good time". So, what this means is that the seriousness of the offense is a consideration that is primarily being applied to non-sex offenders.)

The current application of this consideration as it relates to the circumstance of parole is unjust, in my opinion, as I'll describe by way of the subsequent analogy. As all Americans know, double jeopardy per the 5th amendment is unconstitutional. In other words, someone who is tried and acquitted for a crime cannot be re-tried for the self-same criminal act. Essentially when one is tried and acquitted one's guilt or innocence is considered and determined to the extent that the question is laid to rest. Therefore, the prohibition against making the acquitted face charges repeatedly provides a layer of protection against citizens being burdened with endless ordeals that threaten life and liberty. Through the initial trial of an accused defendant, guilt or innocence is determined and all reasonable jurists subject to the Constitution accept that it's a matter of justice that the question never be probed again following acquittal.

In the case of a defendant who is convicted of a criminal offense, there are also considerations that are applied by a trial court judge at the time of sentencing. One of these many considerations is the seriousness of an offense. Therefore, whatever sentence that an offender serves must have necessarily been imposed after the severity of a criminal act was determined. Hence, the punishment that is inflicted by a trial court judge is in and of itself a consequence of the seriousness of an offense.

What this all means is that since the seriousness of an offense is a consideration that contributes to the sentence imposed it is legally out of order to re-apply the concept as a mechanism to inflict additional punishment at parole hearings. Furthermore, when it comes to the application of the concept by the state parole board its use is akin to an infringement on the jurisdiction given to trial court judges in the sense that they -to the exclusion of other government entities- possess the right to impose a sentence after considering offense seriousness. For people behind bars, it seems as if re-applying this consideration after it was applied by a trial court judge sends the message that the state is willing to violate the premise that led to the constitutional prohibition of double jeopardy. In the state of Tennessee then, the end result of this law has been the weaponization of *'Offense Seriousness'* against worthy parole candidates. Furthermore, it has been the tool that allows prejudiced parole board members to cast life-changing votes arbitrarily.

State parole boards must be forced to limit their functions to assessing the conduct of prisoners while incarcerated, assessing their efforts towards rehabilitation, and assessing the likelihood that an incarcerated person can maintain in society without legal conflict. Some of these factors are enumerated in statute, but when it comes to the application of the law there's a break from what's written. That's the subtlety that has led to our crisis of individual over-incarceration. As Dr. King noted, law can be "...just on its face and unjust in its application." When a parole board denies parole to someone who hasn't done anything to jeopardize the opportunity on the pretext mentioned above, it's safe to say that the decision may be rooted in prejudice or a more sinister state agenda. Anyhow, in the absence of clear legislative directives prohibiting this unjustified conduct it will continue to plague the lives of incarcerated people who have worked at rehabilitation thus diminishing their efforts. The end result of this statute in relation to how prisoners perceive rehabilitative programs and corrections education is that we begin to believe that hard work doesn't count. It creates defiance towards prison authorities because they typically demand us to remain active with work assignments and school while doing time. When a worthy candidate is then denied liberty after self-exertion, the only sentiment re-enforced amongst the incarcerated is that authorities are to be distrusted. Hence, there are many institutions in the state of Tennessee that struggle to get prisoners to come to school and pursue something as essential to life as a G.E.D. Prisoners are having a hard time trusting the efficacy of what's being offered by treatment departments and it all stems from the penal culture that's built around individual over-incarceration and the collateral destruction of morale that it causes. To get a better view of how Tennessee's botched use of this statute works, I conducted some research and interviews with men at the facility I'm located at. I've been in the presence of these men before and after their hearings, so I know the effects of denial all too well. The following are just a few of the stand-up guys I know who've been directly impacted by the unjust application of the *'Offense Seriousness'* statute after serving lengthy amounts of time in prison and doing all the good they can manage to do.

THE PEOPLE WHO'RE OVER-INCARCERATED: THE STORY OF CHRIS ROGERS

Chris Rogers is a well-meaning mentor and R.C.A (Residential Counseling Assistant) in a CBT-based youthful offender program at Northwest Correctional Complex. In the early 1990's he was arrested, tried, and convicted of 1st degree murder in the city of Knoxville, Tennessee. In the aftermath, he was sentenced to a term of life with the possibility of parole. Under the then sentencing code, this meant that he would be eligible for parole after completion of 25 years of imprisonment. At present, he's served 32 calendars after being denied parole on 3 separate occasions. Here's why his incessant denial of freedom is a classic case of over-incarceration through the misuse of T.C.A 40-35-504; Tennessee's legal statute that permits the state parole board to deny parole on the pretext of '*Offense Seriousness*'.

When Chris Rogers walked into the prison system in the early 90's, it was a rough place to live. Violence was the norm, sexual assaults were common, and intoxication was the prevalent form of stress management. Despite these conditions, Chris made the decision to build himself. He took the first step by obtaining his G.E.D. Thereafter, he got involved in trade school where he became a barber and a mentor in cognitive behavior. In the course of time, Chris exemplified amenability to treatment through his willing participation in a vast array of therapeutic programs including, but not limited to, the following: 1) Pro-social life skills, 2) Goal setting awareness,

3) Financial awareness, 4) Fatherhood classes, 5) Carl Perking certifications, 6) CBIB, 7) Therapeutic Community, 8) Manhood series, and 9) Thinking 4 a change. In addition to these things, he also became a part of an inmate organization called P.A.I.I.C.E (Prisoners Actively Involved in Community Endeavors) whose work is to deter youth from crime and make contributions to the welfare of the local community.

As far as institutional behavior is concerned, Rogers has had a number of minor infractions. In 1997, he received a sanction for destruction of state property. In 1999, he failed a urine test for marijuana. In 2013, he received his last disciplinary action for cell phone possession and a failed urine test for marijuana. For the novice there may be no standard to measure his institutional behavior by, but for those who've been within the walls of a prison these discrepancies are insignificant. The remarkable thing is that in a period of 32 years, Chris Rogers has had ***no fights, assaults, or weapons related sanctions***. As of 2023, he's went 10 years without any trouble whatsoever and he consistently works to prevent victimization within the facility that he's housed at.

So, why hasn't Chris Rogers been able to make parole? His record apparently speaks for itself and his risk assessment score reveals that his chances at recidivism are slim to none. Wouldn't he be the ideal candidate for release? Obviously, this is what most reasonable people would believe, but in the state of Tennessee the parole board is not so reasonable. In 2016, he was denied for '*Offense Seriousness*'. The board gave no instruction as to whether or not they wanted him to accomplish more in the way of development, so I think it's safe to say that they personally wanted to see him do a few more years. In 2020, he was once again denied due to '*Offense Seriousness*', but this time he was instructed to complete a period of time in the facility's therapeutic community unit. He humbled himself and did that. In 2022, after compliance with the wishes of the board, he was denied for a 3rd time for the same thing and vaguely instructed to "maintain good institutional behavior". In other words, it was as if the board was saying, "We know that you've done all that you can do and we don't believe that you'll re-offend. Nevertheless, get back into the cage and continue to be a burden on taxpayers." When asked about his thoughts on his continuous denial for the seriousness of the offense Mr. Rogers said, "…I think the parole board uses the tactic to keep people in prison and enhance your sentence by allowing their personal feelings to get involved with the correct decision-making process based on your institutional behavior, programs, and write-ups. The parole board in Tennessee judges and re-sentences people in the system, it's like double jeopardy." When describing how his family felt about his denial he said, "…upset, because they're constantly re-sentencing me over and over again, enhancing my sentence, and I'm not being treated fairly in earning a second chance. When you have a board member telling you you've earned the right for parole, acknowledging your positive behavior, programming, and support systems at the hearing then you receive your final decision in the mail stating you've been denied it's upsetting for you and your family. It makes you feel there's no hope at the end of the tunnel." Powerful words for a board that was created to reward efforts at rehabilitation. The point here is that people who haven't acted in ways that jeopardize their shot at release seemingly have a more difficult time at hearings than those who spend their sentences in non-compliant conduct. It's also important to know that offenders who face serious consequences typically end up displaying more seriousness towards their freedom as can be verified by those familiar with the insides of correctional facilities. Perhaps recidivism can be diminished by giving opportunities to offenders who exhibit the characteristics of the 35% or so that get out never to return to prison.

Chris Rogers is just one of many who've been plagued by the use of the above-mentioned legal weapon. It makes you wonder why the general public isn't asking the question, "Why do all the '*wrong people*' keep getting relief from incarceration?" The consideration of *offense seriousness over positive maturation* is one of the reasons.

THE PEOPLE WHO'RE OVER-INCARCERATED: THE STORY OF CEDRIC PHELPS

Cedric Phelps is a concerned son, father, and grandfather who is 48 years old. In 1996, he was tried and convicted of 1st degree murder in the small town of Clarksville, TN. As a result, he was sentenced to a term of life in prison with parole eligibility after a minimum of 25 years served. At present, he's done almost 27 years after being denied release on the pretext of *'Offense Seriousness'*. Here's why his denial of parole defies logic and is another example of Tennessee's tendency to keep the *'right'* people incarcerated.

Cedric "Ced" Phelps is a structured military veteran, so when he arrived in Tennessee's prison system the environment was an aberration from what he was accustomed to. In those days, prisons were heavily influenced by gangs. This meant that chaos and violence was commonplace. In one instance, Mr. Phelps even found himself the victim of a botched gang hit as he innocently came out of a prison library. Fortunately for him, he had friends around who rushed him to the institutional clinic before he bled out or developed an infection. Sounds like a lot to deal with, right? Amazingly enough, he persevered and his resilience manifested in the form of self-application in the midst of unpredictable surroundings.

In his first decade of incarceration, Cedric made the decision to become an expert craftsman. He took action by enrolling in vocational school where he took up welding, commercial cleaning, and small engines. His philosophy while progressing through these classes was to keep in mind that the more that he learned, the more options he would have to succeed when he made it back home. Needless to say, he successfully completed each class making it a point to help countless students along the way. In his more recent years of incarceration he went through Barber College, becoming a licensed barber as determined by the state board. The trade intrigued him when his son became inclined to it, so they fed off of each other as they pursued their licenses. The only difference between the two now is that his son is running a successful barbershop on the outside while he works for change at the barbershop at Northwest Correctional Complex. At present, he's working towards obtaining his instructor's license in the field, so he'll be ready if he ever gets the opportunity to work as an instructor. Outside of trade school, Mr. Phelps enrolled in college courses. In a few short months, he'll have the honor of walking across the stage as a proud business school graduate of Lane College- a school in Jackson, TN. An opportunity that was made possible in Tennessee prisons by the Tennessee Higher Education Initiative in recent years.

Considering the subtle effects of incarceration, Cedric found it wise to seek out the various therapeutic services that were within his reach. He wanted to tend to his overall well-being and learn something that he could pass on to his children and grandchildren in the process. Therefore, he participated in the following programs, becoming proficient in their content: 1) Anger Management, 2) Victim's Impact, 3) Thinking 4 a Change, 4) NA/AA, and 5) CMS-Career Management for

Success. The sum total of his efforts being the production of a man who has all the tools necessary to get out and maintain in society without conflict with the law.

As far as institutional behavior is concerned, Cedric Phelps has a few minor sanctions that can be called outright silly. In 1998, he was written up for 'interfering with officer duties' because he fell asleep during a sitting or standing prison head count after he came back from the hospital under the effects of medication. In 2004, he received a sanction for 'contraband' after being caught with sliced cheese in his cell and in the same year he was disciplined for being "out of place." In 2005, he was again written up for 'contraband' after being caught with a pair of paper scissors that he used to make homemade holiday cards with. In 2018, he received his last disciplinary action for being in possession of a few cigarettes, earning him another 'contraband' sanction. By prison standards then, it can be said that Cedric has been the model prisoner. **He hasn't been caught with any weapons, he hasn't assaulted any officers, he's not involved with gangs, and he hasn't been involved with the prison drug trade. Things that are all too common in Tennessee's prison system**. So the question begs itself, why didn't Cedric Phelps make parole when his hearing was conducted? As was the case with Chris Rogers, *'Offense Seriousness'* was the catalyst.

On December 21, 2021 Mr. Phelps prepared to go meet the state parole board. After all of the work that he'd done throughout his sentence, he believed that his chances were high. Furthermore, he was approaching 50 years of age and he'd served over a quarter of a century. To his delight, his family was there to support him and go to bat for him as necessary. As the hearing began, things were seemingly going well. Mention was made of his case, but his development was beginning to dominate the conversation. Things took a turn for the worst when it came time for an ex-law enforcement member of the parole board to speak. From the outset, he revealed his prejudice by displaying unjustified suspicion against a confused Mr. Phelps. From there, he fixated on the crime to the extent of disregarding the programming, behavior, and educational achievements that were directly in front of him. Unfortunately for Cedric, his assessment was enough to thwart Mr. Phelps from getting the votes necessary to make parole. In the end he was put off for an additional 3 years.

When asked if he believed that his hearing was free of prejudice, Phelps replied, "No. When you have a former homicide detective sitting on the parole board listening to a murder case it's almost like a re-trial." A reference to the questionable board member selection in the state of Tennessee. According to his final decision that he later received in the mail, the reason for his denial was *'Offense Seriousness'* and he was also vaguely instructed to maintain "good institutional behavior." A slap in the face for a man who had done everything in his power not to jeopardize his opportunity at release. The instruction given was thus, in my opinion, acknowledgement of the fact that Cedric Phelps would've been the ideal parole candidate. The board just couldn't overcome the dictates of vengeance and were thus blinded to the fact that Mr. Phelps had already endured punishment for over 25 years! An amount of punishment that any objective thinker would duly consider.

When asked how his family felt about the decision Mr. Phelps revealed, "They were hurt because they wanted me home." In reference to T.C.A 40-35-503, the state statute on *'Offense Seriousness'* he went on to say, "Seriousness of the offense is just a tool used to keep people here. They don't look at the change in a person, just the charge." The next hearing for Cedric Phelps is in 2024, by then he'll be finished with his Bachelor's degree in Business Administration. Only time will tell how the parole board decides his case. His situation adds additional clarity on how a person who comes to prison to get worse can have priority over a man who exhibits positive maturation in the sight of Tennessee's parole board.

THE PEOPLE WHO'RE OVER-INCARCERATED: THE STORY OF ROBERT HOWELL

Robert L. Howell is a soft-spoken senior who's simply striving for a shot at release so that he can live out the remainder of his years without the stress of being in prison. In 1992, he was convicted of 1st degree murder and was thereafter sentenced to a term of life in prison with the possibility of parole after a minimum of 25 calendars. At present, he's done 32 years straight and he's anticipating his next meeting with the board which is scheduled for August of 2023. The tragedy in this case is that he's been denied parole on 3 separate occasions for *'Offense Seriousness'* as enumerated under T.C.A 40-35-503 when his conduct shows that he has essentially aged out of crime.

In the early 90's, life in prison was tense. There were no cameras, prisoners had the ability to move freely within institutional grounds, and race prejudice was rampant. To say that a young white male like Robert Howell had to be careful would be an understatement. Furthermore, his background of poverty meant that his family couldn't provide the financial backing necessary to ease the pangs of being incarcerated. In other words, survival was the name of the game and since Mr. Howell is still here and functioning mentally it's safe to say that he has the ability to survive without resorting to anything truly blameworthy. This has been the case even when the going gets rough.

Throughout his sentence, Mr. Howell has been the ideal of employment consistency in an environment where people generally avoid work and jump from job-to-job reflecting an inability to be stable. Early in his sentence, he discovered that he loved to cook. As a result, that's what he's done for 24 of his 32 years of confinement. His work as a cook has done him a lot of good, since a plate of decent food here and there can be exchanged for basic necessities in an environment like prison. From what I've witnessed myself, it's a pity that Mr. Howell's cooking skills aren't being showcased at some restaurant. It's as if the state wants to use him up and then release him when he has no abilities left. In the event of that happening, he'll simply leave prison where he was a burden to taxpayers to continue as the same in the free world. Wouldn't it be better to let him out while he still has abilities left, so that he can finally contribute to society in some way?

In recent years, Mr. Howell has been engaged in therapeutic programming. As a matter of fact, he's went through the following courses: 1) CMS (Career Management for Success), 2) Anger Management, 3) C.B.I.P (Cognitive Behavior Initiative Program) where he was recognized as a positive influencer, 4) NA/AA, 5) Victim's Impact, and 6) Thinking 4 a Change. He's done all of these things in efforts to better prepare for society. After 3 decades he knows the world has changed, so he's gearing up to adjust to it.

While in prison, Robert has received a mere 8 disciplinary sanctions. Mostly minor infractions such as unauthorized financial transactions, possession of tobacco, and a couple of larceny sanctions he received after being caught exchanging food items from the institutional kitchen for his basic necessities off of commissary... something that prison frequently calls upon needy men to do. In the early 90's, he caught a write-up for possession of a deadly weapon in an era where you'd rather get caught with it than without it. The important thing about his conduct while locked up is that he's had **no violent encounters, he's no drug dealer, and he's not an addict.** He's simply an older man who's learned how to roll with the punches and think before he rushes into action. Now he's spending his days wondering why men who've spent their sentences engaged in bloodshed are being let out before him. A puzzling question to say the least.

At this point I bet you're wondering, 'Why hasn't Robert been able to make parole?' According to the parole board *'Offense Seriousness'* is the answer. In July of 2015, he was set off for 6 years. In July of 2021, he was set off for a year. In August of 2022, he was again set off for a year and he's currently scheduled to go and see the board in August of 2023. An important part of these hearings has been the presence of protesters. In other words, family members of the deceased victim have come to express their desire to see Mr. Howell die in prison. Undoubtedly, this fact has played a major part in the board's decision to deny him parole. The fact that Mr. Howell turned to rehabilitative programs in close proximity to his parole date and after his initial rejection may have been an issue as well. Nevertheless, we must think to ourselves as a society, 'Is the criminal justice system designed to seek out vengeance or justice?' In the event of crime, there will always be affected parties who're unable to forgive or at least move on with their lives and leave bitterness in the past. Is it then fair for taxpayers to keep bearing the burden of vengeance exacted, or is there a time when the system should factor in the welfare of the state in general and take action to stop the punishment? I'll allow you to decide that for yourself. What's apparent in the case of Robert Howell is that the parole board has seemingly allowed vengeance to rule the day. It's my humble, concerned opinion that the time to let up has come and gone. At current his rejections are like kicks to a man that's already down.

(*Note: In Aug. of 2023, Robert Howell went up for parole and was denied. He appealed the decision and the matter ended up before a middle Tennessee Chancery Court where misapplication of the law on the part of the parole board was uncovered. There was never a formal determination in the case, but there was seemingly a court directive that caused the board to backtrack and give Mr. Howell a 2024 release date.)

WHAT OFFENDERS THINK WHEN WE ASSESS PAROLE DETERMINATIONS:

In the course of living, we all hear the statement "*The only thing that's constant is change*." While doing time and striving to take advantage of the things that are considered to be avenues of rehabilitation, - i.e. programs, vocational classes, higher education, etc.-, one of the many psychological struggles that you encounter is the reality that the general public has very little faith in the idea that change and growth applies to incarcerated people just as it applies to them. In here, your day to day reality is plagued by the possibility that irrespective of what you do now and have done consistently for years, the state and all of its constituents receive you according to who you were in the midst of criminal patterns or a single criminal act. When it comes to incarcerated people it's as if natural development, maturity, and moral growth are not on the table. In the eyes of the incarcerated, parole denials such as the denials that I've just provided serve to re-enforce these sentiments. For example, when asked if he believed that his strivings were duly considered after he was denied parole for the 3rd time, Eric Miller responded with a vehement "NO!" He further stated, "…them telling me to keep doing as I have been doing was sort of an acknowledgement, but when I found out that they gave parole to another lifer who had 5 write-ups in the previous year, it made me wonder what the point of bettering myself was. That made me angry."

As it relates to above-mentioned circumstances, it seems as if decisions are made in accord with the emotional state of parole board members at the time that they make decisions. If not, how can a man who is seemingly destined for recidivism be given release priority over someone whom records indicate will appreciate the opportunity in word and deed? Perhaps the judging of prisoners by people who've never set foot within a correctional institution needs to be stopped. People who have no in-house experience inevitably make decisions rooted in a lack of knowledge of how prisoners phase through criminality in an abnormal environment like prison. Unfortunately, statutes such as the *'Offense Seriousness'* law exacerbate the problem.

In recent years, Tennessee's parole board has become even more intense in its commitment to confinement. As a result, the state's parole release rate is diminishing.

Here are the numbers:

	2019	**2020**	**2021**	**2022**
Number of parole board decisions	14,344	13,787	11,934	11,441
Number of people granted parole	4,984	4,742	3,872	3,150
Parole grant rate	34.70%	34.40%	32.40%	27.50%

Source: Prison Policy Initiative

This information shows that the people I speak for will have to withstand parole denial even when their institutional record shows that they haven't done anything that calls for it. A reality that has prompted many social commentators to call the prison system an "industrial complex" since it seems as if states have an agenda to keep prisoners as long as possible in order to make as much money as possible off of them while they can. Whether this is true or false, my stance is that lawmakers must produce legislation that makes parole a presumptive matter…a presumption given, of course, with the consideration that exceptional circumstances tend to exist. Either way, we can't slow down individual over-incarceration until our *'Offense Seriousness'* utilization is severely limited.

SECTION 2

The People Who're Over-Incarcerated

By way of '*Extensive Sentences*'

EXTENSIVE SENTENCES

The broader demographic of prisoners who're over-incarcerated are serving extensive sentences; sentences that require service of more than 20 calendars of confinement with no meaningful mechanism for obtaining relief besides the current 'Good Time' distribution system. Life without parole sentences, life with parole sentences, extensive sentences that come from stacked charges, and sentences in accord with Tennessee's career criminal statute are some of the sentence types responsible for the lengthy stays in prison that preclude a chance at earning relief for progressive minded prisoners in desperation. The following are just a few out of dozens of extraordinary men who would benefit from the construction of a meaningful mechanism that could be applied to extensive sentences in reward for growth and an unwavering commitment to the righting of wrongs.

(***Note**: The Tennessee legislature, to the shock of many prisoners, recently enacted the 'Truth in Sentencing Act.' This law expands the use of true 100% sentences thereby eliminating the chance to earn 'Good Time' for many incoming prisoners. In laymen's terms, this means prisoners sentenced under this law have very little incentive to go to school, work, or any of the programs associated with rehabilitation. The 'Truth in Sentencing Act' will undoubtedly contribute to Tennessee's crisis of individual over-incarceration.)

THE PEOPLE WHO'RE OVER- INCARCERATED: HOWARD COLEMAN

Howard Coleman is a 51 year old man who's been incarcerated for over 26 years. He's currently serving a life sentence without the possibility of parole and although he seemingly has no incentive to do the right thing, he's managed to make strides within himself. Here's his story in his own words:

"On July 12, 1997 my friends and I enjoyed the day as usual. Back then, we spent our days in laughter and the consumption of marijuana and alcohol. That was our way of escaping the realities of the poor streets of Memphis. After following the script that day, we decided to go to the store to purchase additional alcoholic beverages. As we traversed an alleyway, we were approached by a man known to one of my friends. As fate would have it, he was looking for some gambling buddies. On that note, one of my then friends mischievously ran across the street to retrieve a gun unbeknownst to the rest of us. I guess he connected the dots and concluded that a man looking to gamble would be in possession of money. I wasn't so swift, considering the fact that I didn't rob people regularly. As this took place, the man who ultimately became our victim went to a nearby store for a moment. This is when my now armed friend returned to the group with the suggestion that we rob the man when he came back to the scene. My first inclination upon hearing this talk was to leave, but false loyalty and peer pressure overcame me with the result that I stayed. In retrospect, I rationalized this decision of mine with the idea that if I took the gun and controlled the situation nothing drastic would happen…boy was I wrong. When the victim returned, we all surrounded him as I raised the weapon towards him amidst my friends hollering 'Give up the money!' As my adrenaline level rose from being in a foreign circumstance, I hastily reacted and fired 2 shots at the victim. As he retreated, I fired 3 more shots causing him to tumble to the ground. From there, my friends and I took his possessions and fled the scene. Later that day, my charge partners were arrested and on the following day, I too was apprehended. Now, I'm a quarter of a century removed from the crime and still wrestling with the consequences.

Throughout my initial years of incarceration, my life continued to be out of control. As a newcomer to prison, I was angry with myself and I directed it towards others at times. I was housed at the high-custody site at Northwest Correctional Complex where I was surrounded by gang members who essentially ran the prison. Influenced by my conditioning on the streets, the prison environment, and the loss of hope that my sentence brought, I developed a sense of rebelliousness to authority and an aversion to change that caused me to have disciplinary issues. Remarkably though, I managed to get my points down and I ended up being given a chance to move to the low-custody site of the facility where things were less crime oriented. I know it may sound odd, but I was unable to adjust to the more peaceful living quarters which resulted in my transfer back to the high-custody side of the institution. This ping-pong between sites continued for a while until one day I finally had enough and on my last trip to the high-custody side I sincerely began to evaluate myself inside and out. I realized that I had a family that loved me and it was my duty to at least love them back enough to value my own wellbeing.

Thereafter, I became more involved with the church and regular in my Bible study. This became the source of encouragement that prompted me to make the changes that I knew were necessary. I began by obtaining my G.E.D, thereby producing a little bit of confidence within me that I could probably accomplish more if I applied my intellect. I then took it upon myself to become proficient in several trades, namely Carpentry and HVAC/Refrigeration mechanics where I received an E.P.A license to practice within the industry.

With consideration for my traumatic upbringing and the things I'd seen and dealt with in prison, I knew it would be constructive for me to open myself up to therapy. I then enrolled in therapeutic programs like the Cognitive Behavior Initiative Program, Career Management for Success, Victim's Impact, and NA/AA. I went on to become a member of P.A.I.I.C.E (Prisoners Actively Involved in Community Endeavors) and this is something that I'm particularly proud of. Through the organization's 'Don't Follow Me' program, I get to express to local children that a life of crime is something to avoid which brings me a satisfaction that I truly can't explain.

As a mature man, I feel remorse for the life that I took everyday. I realize the collateral damage that I brought to the family of the victim, my own family, and the neighborhood that I should've strived to uplift. I can't change the past, but I have to say that I wouldn't trade the lessons I've learned from it for anything. What I can say is that I'm totally devoted to living a life without legal conflict and should I make it out, my skills will be employed to prevent crimes like the crime that I committed from occurring in the future. If I re-capture my freedom my goals are to practice the trades that I know, spend some time with my aging mother, and continue my involvement with P.A.I.I.C.E. In the meantime, I'll continue my progress by striving for admission into the college program here at N.W.C.X. I think the best way to atone for my misdeeds is through ensuring that I evolve as far away from crime as possible. Everything I do reflects that belief."

As an 18 year-old coming into general population from the juvenile housing unit, I had the good fortune of meeting Howard Coleman. In a place filled with addiction and gang activity, he took it upon himself to personally encourage me to act upon the good intentions that I had formulated. I wouldn't be the man I am today without him and I consider it a privilege to try to let the world know that there is an 'inside consensus' on the fact that he's a man who needs a chance. Who he is today would prompt just about anyone who gets to know him to have mercy on him if they had the power to do so.

THE PEOPLE WHO'RE OVER-INCARCERATED: GRADY "HABIB" THOMAS

Grady "Habib" Thomas is a friendly 53 year old man from Memphis, TN. At present, he's been incarcerated for 27 years in connection with an incident that took place in September of '96. An incident that was preceded by a complicated sequence of events that included an attempted robbery of Mr. Thomas and a subsequent nightclub confrontation that unfortunately led to today's consequences of heartache and confinement… confinement inflicted by the state as a consequence for 2 counts of 1st degree murder that were raised against Mr. Thomas. In the aftermath, Mr. Thomas was convicted by way of a plea deal requiring the imposition of 2 concurrent life sentences with the possibility of parole. He's served most of his sentence at Northwest Correctional Complex where he's dealt with the situation honorably to say the least.

When he entered the prison system, Mr. Thomas embarked upon the journey of self-improvement. He began by tending to his faith and learning how to be true to it since the actions of people rest upon their beliefs. In his own words, "Since my incarceration, I have focused on religion as a tool for self-reformation." His focus within the pursuit of righteousness therefore has led to his consistent involvement as a teacher of the facility's Islamic services where he's served for more than 20 years. In addition to this, Mr. Thomas decided to get into therapy. This led to his enrollment in Cage Your Rage group therapy sessions which he gained immense benefit from in the late 90's.

Despite dealing with a lengthy sentence, Mr. Thomas went on to further his academic level and professional skills. He got into plumbing, successfully completing an apprenticeship/vocational course. He then absorbed himself into leatherwork and at present he's capable of producing custom high-quality belts, purses, handbags, etc. If he's blessed with release from prison, the plan is to open a leather goods establishment and earn a living with his hands. Perhaps the most impressive thing about Mr. Thomas is his academic record. According to Thomas himself, "In 2017, I enrolled in the college program with the Tennessee Higher Education Initiative and earned an Associate's Degree from Dyersburg State Community College. I graduated as co-valedictorian with honors and a 4.0 G.P.A. Furthermore, I went on to earn a Bachelor's degree in Business Administration from Lane College thereby making history as a part of the first cohort to do so in Tennessee's prisons. I also maintained a 4.0 G.P.A and graduated with honors from Lane College." This stellar record of accomplishments reveals one fact to any keen observer...Grady Thomas is true in his evolution as a man, especially when we consider that his sentence makes material benefit distant on the horizon.

Admittedly, Grady Thomas was once a man worthy of arrest, accountability, and perhaps the sentence that he received. Nevertheless, he's matured into a man worthy of mercy, freedom, and a chance to assist in the fight to keep our fellow Tennesseans out of prison. He says, "I regret what I did and I am sorry for my actions. I hurt a lot of people including the victims' families and my family. Regardless of the situation, I had no right to take someone's life. Furthermore, the lifestyle that I was living was wrong. As a consequence, I have taken deliberate steps to change my behavior and way of thinking." In my years of incarceration, I would say that Habib has been instrumental to the progress of scores of men. Without a doubt, he's a leader amongst the small group of prisoners that have grown into the qualities that produce successful re-entry. His case is therefore clearly within the scope of individual over-incarceration and his self-application makes him a prime candidate for re-assessment if we ever decide to start releasing the *'right'* people into society. The icing on the cake in this instance is that Mr. Thomas has managed to execute the near impossible feat of avoiding a single disciplinary infraction in over a quarter century of confinement! A true miracle, especially when all of the things that could go wrong in a prison are considered. It's safe to say that most citizens of the state- if they knew of our current, misguided release practices- would rather have a man like Mr. Thomas next door as opposed to someone who has no concept of getting out, staying out, or being productive. Mr. Thomas, therefore, is an example of the seriousness towards life that comes from wrestling with serious adversity.

THE PEOPLE WHO'RE OVER-INCARCERATED: TUT M. TUT

With criticism and objectivity in mind, I've contemplated whether or not to include myself within the category of prisoners who're over-incarcerated. I don't think anyone wants to come off as self-righteous or entitled to anything, especially in relation to things that other people ultimately have the position to decide anyway. Nevertheless, I'm simply a human being trying to survive a hostile environment, so I can't betray my survival instincts and fail to convey my own maturation story while growing up in the prison system. If I was asked about what I've determined within myself I'd say that I'm at a place where I understand my connection to others, I understand how to love myself, and I'm true to the respect I've gained for the rights of others. Because of this, I'm not afraid to say that if I end up serving this entire sentence it's my belief that I'll wind up being caught up in our over-incarceration machine like the rest of my comrades. The question then is whether or not you, as an intelligent reader, can make a clear determination based upon who records indicate I've become.

Those who know me now might find it difficult to reconcile who I am at present with who I was in the past. Time, pressure, accountability, and abnormal circumstances have led me to become something other than what I was. In the early morning hours of March 17, 2012 my three co-defendants and I were involved in a kidnapping and robbery that escalated into a torture situation. We're all related and I'm the youngest of the four. At the time I was merely 15 years old. On that life-changing night, one of my charge partners and I initiated the crime by aggressively attacking the two male victims thereby causing one of them to react with resistance. As a matter of fact, he splashed me with a cup of hot coffee and a tussle ensued. At the time I was an impulsive robber with an entitlement complex and I was at a stage in my life where I lived in pursuit of notoriety. Furthermore, my judgment was always clouded by my consumption of marijuana, alcohol, and prescription pills… my three older cousins were no different. These components of who I was caused me to feel offended and disrespected by the resistance of the victim, so we proceeded to beat and stab both of them repeatedly. In the midst of the chaos I thought to myself, 'What's the worst thing I can do to these two guys short of killing them?" Thereafter, I forced one victim to take the other victim's genitals into his mouth and vice versa. It was about humiliation. I was so far gone at the time that I had a backwards sense of accomplishment with the bloodshed and degradation I'd carried out. In my distorted view of things, I was growing into the criminal figure that people would avoid conflict with. I really believed at the time that my way was the way to avoiding victimization and accumulating respect, so I committed crimes that reflected an urge to make a name for myself in the underworld.

A couple of days later -on March 19, 2012- I was arrested and charged with multiple counts of kidnapping, robbery, and rape. I ended up being transferred to adult criminal court where I was indicted and convicted by way of a plea agreement for a sentence of 30 years. I was 16 years old when I arrived in state prison with an inability to fathom getting out and having the shot to become a productive adult. After all, I didn't have any experience with adult living on the outside, the juvenile courts considered me to be beyond repair, and I was wrestling with the demoralizing effect of having the convictions that I had knowing full well that I hadn't had any illegal sexual contact with anyone. Nevertheless, I was in the jungle now and I couldn't allow myself to become absorbed in self-pity. I wasn't the only kid in the system, I wasn't the only person to face excess in prosecutorial tactics, and I damn sure wasn't the first person to suffer for his ignorance. I was absorbing my first lesson on the divine law of consequences and I was slowly waking up to the moral realities that I'd always heard of, but never really believed in. I guess there was something in me that compelled me to go forward even when my mind couldn't see anything in front of me.

By the time that I arrived in the TDOC, I had begun to sink deeper into different viewpoints. The blow of accountability that came with facing a lifetime of incarceration humbled me and I really began to feed into my good side. I knew that the things that I admired, the things that I did, and the man that I aspired to be prior to incarceration was poisonous. At the facility that I ended up in, I had the good fortune of going through a C.B.T (Cognitive Behavioral Therapy)-based program for youth. As fate would have it, I met an old counselor by the name of Dr. Welch who really cared about those of us he worked with and through his challenges my ability to assess my old way of thinking grew and my old, detrimental ideology no longer was the only way of seeing things. Through therapy, I was exposed to stress management techniques, violence prevention techniques, and pro-social life skills. I would say that my early exposure to change and my receptiveness to therapy was the catalyst for the milestones that I managed to reach thereafter.

As a teenager, I obtained my G.E.D. A few years later, I received my Associate's degree in Business Administration from Dyersburg State Community College and I continued my studies until I obtained my Bachelor's degree in Business Administration from Lane College. As a matter of fact, I was the leader of the first male cohort to ever earn 4-year degrees in Tennessee's prison system, making history alongside of Grady "Habib" Thomas. It was never easy, but life had literally prepared me for difficulty and prison life made me long-suffering. Therefore, I've grown to live a life characterized by the words of Denzel Washington, "Ease is a greater threat to progress than difficulty." It's my belief that the power of a good intention attracts elements that are aligned with success. The opportunities that have seemingly materialized at my feet are a testament to that.

While furthering myself academically, I also took up trades and became a craftsman. I went through Electrical, HVAC/Refrigeration mechanics, and Barber College where I received my Master Barber's license and my E.P.A license in refrigerant use. I took craftsmanship to be important due to my lack of experience with adult living on the outside, so in my mind I needed skills that would contribute to my ability to function in society without being dependent upon others. While doing time, people you know naturally fade away and if you have a lengthy sentence even family begins to count you out. Regardless of this though, its been my job to accept responsibility for my actions while taking on the simultaneous responsibility I have to constantly improve my circumstances. With this attitude on my heart, I've matured into someone that can be trusted to do the right thing by others and take care of my fundamental responsibilities as a man.

In retrospect, I would say that I was probably one of the most dangerous criminals on the street. Not a day goes by that I don't look into the past and wish that I could prevent myself from doing the things that I did to the victims on the night that I committed this crime. As a matter of fact, I wrestle with feelings about all of the crimes I've committed... a reality that I recently had to reckon with upon the death of my cousin and my charge partner, Duol T. Wal. I can't tell you what the future holds for me, but I'm ready to live a new life on the outside with the respect I've gained for the rights of others. Out of all of the components to who I am now, the most important is that my moral fiber detests circulating the pain that I used to circulate. Because of this, what I do and who I am isn't about dodging government sanction or a hatred for the discomfort of imprisonment. It's about realizing how connected I really am to my brothers and sisters in the world and **not doing unto others what I wouldn't have done to myself**. When I make it through this sentence my goals are to utilize my education in the workforce, exercise my craft as a barber, and work my way into the coffee industry. On a more personal level I intend to re-learn my family members, progress as an author, and contribute to the improvement of the criminal justice system.

At present, I'm in an ongoing legal battle with the state of Tennessee. To my surprise, my sentence was altered by my trial court to reflect a plea deal that I didn't agree to. The issue being a result of an error on the part of the D.A.'s office that I'm unfortunately being punished for with an additional 4 and half years of time…a period of time that may mean nothing to practitioners of our legal system and absolutely everything to a man like me. If it's in the lord's will though, I'll prevail in court and at least have my sentence reverted back to the terms that I lent my signature to. There's also hope for me in 2022's Tyshon Booker case, considering the fact that Tennessee's Supreme Court adopted language from our nation's high court in relation to juvenile offenders being sentenced in adult court. The case specifically addressed mandatory life sentences in homicide cases, but I believe it will eventually produce change for youthful offenders convicted in non-homicide cases as well. I guess I'll find out soon though, as I attempt to deal with my ongoing legal troubles.

STEPPING AWAY FROM OVER-INCARCERATION

In the process of de-constructing the elements of our legal system that lead to over-incarceration, it's important to usher in a new era of practice characterized by the utilization of expertise when assessing prisoners. In fact, this is done throughout the country albeit in various degrees and in different ways. The state of Tennessee however, is on the weak end of this already deficient national spectrum while suffering from a labor force that is extremely short, grossly incompetent, and handicapped by the nepotism that prevents qualified candidates from gaining positions that they actually know how to work. If the acquisition of experts ever becomes a fact, I believe that the government would have to follow up by forming an agency or re-assessment board with the specific task of identifying prisoners serving extensive sentences that have earned the right to be at least considered for release by virtue of their development, works, and accomplishments. A rational course of action that is distinct from men and women being indiscriminately handed relief from sentences without demonstrated proof of abandoning Anti-Social Personality Disorder.

To make it more clear, in the Department of Correction there are 2 categories of people: **1.) Prisoners serving non-extensive sentences** and **2.) Prisoners serving extensive sentences**. *Non-extensive sentences* are sentences that require service of 20 calendars maximum. In other words, sentences that require an individual to serve 20 years or less. *Extensive* *sentences* are sentences that require service of more than 20 calendars of incarceration with no meaningful mechanism of relief besides Tennessee's current system of '"Good Time" distribution. These sentences include the various life sentences as well as sentences that possess an apparent release eligibility date (R.E.D), albeit after completion of 20 years of confinement. The identification of these specific classes of offenders is important because over-incarceration, in most cases, occurs to individuals serving extensive sentences. These are the types of prisoners that a Tennessee seeking to improve would have to begin to consider.

Therefore, with the creation of the above-mentioned government entity, there would have to be safeguards in place to ensure that decisions are free from bias and corruption. Currently, our legal system's decisions are smitten with political agendas, pseudo-science, and the tendency to cater to some of the more unrefined parts of our nation's history. With this reality in mind, those charged with addressing over-incarceration would have to be as far removed from politics and the corporate world as possible. When this happens, we can then establish this beacon of hope for prisoners while generating additional motivation for our incarcerated citizens to engage in productive activity within the prison system.

The most significant tool that I envision for the above-mentioned agency would be the **E.R.E.D, or the Earned Release Eligibility Date**... a discretionary tool that would distribute release opportunities to individuals who decide to approach life with serious self-examination after conviction.

The E.R.E.D would directly and indirectly affect recidivism, prison overcrowding, and phase our legal system away from the status quo of cruelty that typically backfires in the long run. In my experience, prison culture is heavily influenced by prisoners serving extensive sentences. Therefore, if legitimate chances for release are placed on the horizon for these kinds of offenders those serving non-extensive sentences stand to benefit from the culture shift that will naturally ensue. In other words, the efforts at development that long-term prisoners put forth will permeate institutions ultimately affecting prisoners with shorter sentences. It all depends on citizens of Tennessee standing up and speaking out against the silent doctrines of incorrigibility that we accord to convicted felons though. It pains me to be the bearer of bad news, but the truth is that we'll all probably have someone we love within the clutches of our justice system at some point or another. If they choose to get themselves together in the process wouldn't you want the system to have a way to dish out some grace? Because of this reality then, I request that you use your voice to promote the idea of establishing a government entity that re-assesses people serving extensive sentences. I ask that you use your voice to circulate the necessity of the E.R.E.D. As the story of Jonah teaches, there are times when problems can only be corrected by people who've been inside the belly of the whale. Over-incarceration, unfortunately, is a force that stifles the full extent of the change that our hidden change makers can truly make.

CONCLUSION

The crisis of individual over-incarceration we've created is not something that we can afford to overlook or approach with indifference. We're all inextricably intertwined and as Dr. King wrote in his famous letter from the Birmingham jail, "Injustice anywhere is a threat to justice everywhere." In this context, this means that the veiled cruelties of our justice system are closer to home than you may think. In America, the truth is that the story of being a prisoner is seldom one where you're apprehended, punished, and that's the end of the story. There's seemingly always another method used to twist the knife... methods that are a manifestation of our unforgiving punitive culture, our deficient practices when assessing culpability, and our sub-conscious ideas about who has value in our society and who doesn't. Whether it's through unjust parole board actions through the use of the *'Offense Seriousness'* statue, setting up life sentences with unattainable parole dates, or stacking charges in criminal cases with the result of consecutive sentences; citizens behind bars who strive for success post-release are literally collecting dust in corrections institutions... institutions that are akin to fulfillment centers where the product never leaves. I say all of this as a man who believes in law, order, and accountability when applied with pure objectives. The difference is that I temper this with my belief in the use of justice over vengeance and the administration of mercy to those who're penitent.

As a society we have to ask ourselves, what harm would there be if we shifted into this perspective and tried to introduce this mindset into our legal system? Recidivism statistics -to the detriment of our communities- show that we're giving mercy to the *'wrong'* people anyway! The time to re-distribute opportunities to the *'right'* people then is now. It's my sincere prayer that common citizens begin to think about our veiled prison society and the trauma, victimization, and depraved living conditions that lead people into the commission of crime… the real issues that are seldom investigated and addressed by competent professionals. I think our general lack of thought when it comes to these issues is what fuels our lack of compassion with the incarcerated in a world that's rife with distractions. At the end of the day, we're all more alike than we would like to think and that's whether we're incarcerated or not. It would probably surprise you to know how many corrections officers tell me after spending time with prisoners, "I could've been right here with you." I'll leave off with a quote from Thomas Merton that provides insight into how healing is only possible through compassion…healing that individual over-incarceration doesn't generate for our communities:

"We are bodies of broken bones. I guess I'd always known but never fully considered that being broken is what makes us human. We all have our reasons. Sometimes we're fractured by the choices we make; sometimes we're shattered by the things we would have never chosen. But our brokenness is also the source of our common humanity, the basis for our shared search for comfort, meaning, and healing. Our shared vulnerability and imperfection nurtures and sustains our capacity for compassion."

Perhaps acknowledging the existence of individual over-incarceration will be a starting point for making our prison system a real 'Department of Correction'. For now though, let's begin by addressing Tennessee's ***'Offense Seriousness'*** statute and our use of ***'Extensive Sentences'*** that have no meaningful mechanism for relief that can be applied to them.

www.ingramcontent.com/pod-product-compliance
Lightning Source LLC
LaVergne TN
LVHW090433210926
848480LV00002B/806

* 9 7 9 8 2 3 2 7 4 8 8 0 7 *